# BENCHMARK LITERACY

## Grade 1
## Texts for Close Reading

## Table of Contents

| Unit 1 | 3 |
| Unit 2 | 17 |
| Unit 3 | 35 |
| Unit 4 | 49 |
| Unit 5 | 63 |
| Unit 6 | 77 |
| Unit 7 | 91 |
| Unit 8 | 105 |
| Unit 9 | 119 |
| Unit 10 | 133 |

# Unit 1

## Table of Contents

Signs . . . . . . . . . . . . . . . . 4

Community Helpers . . . . . . . . . . . 5

Light. . . . . . . . . . . . . . . . . 6

Habitats Around the World. . . . . . . . 7

Things I Like to Do . . . . . . . . . . .16

# Signs

Reading road signs is easy if you look at their colors.

Red means "stop."

Yellow means "be careful."

Orange signs let us know that people are working on the road.

# Community Helpers

Many people have jobs helping other people. Police officers keep people safe. Firefighters get people out of burning buildings and put out fires. Doctors help people stay healthy. Sick people go to the doctor to get better, too.

Would you like to help people when you grow up? What would you like to do?

# Light

Many things give us light. The sun gives us most of our light. Light from the sun is very bright. Fire gives us light. Big fires give more light than little fires. Lightbulbs use electricity to give us light. What other things give us light?

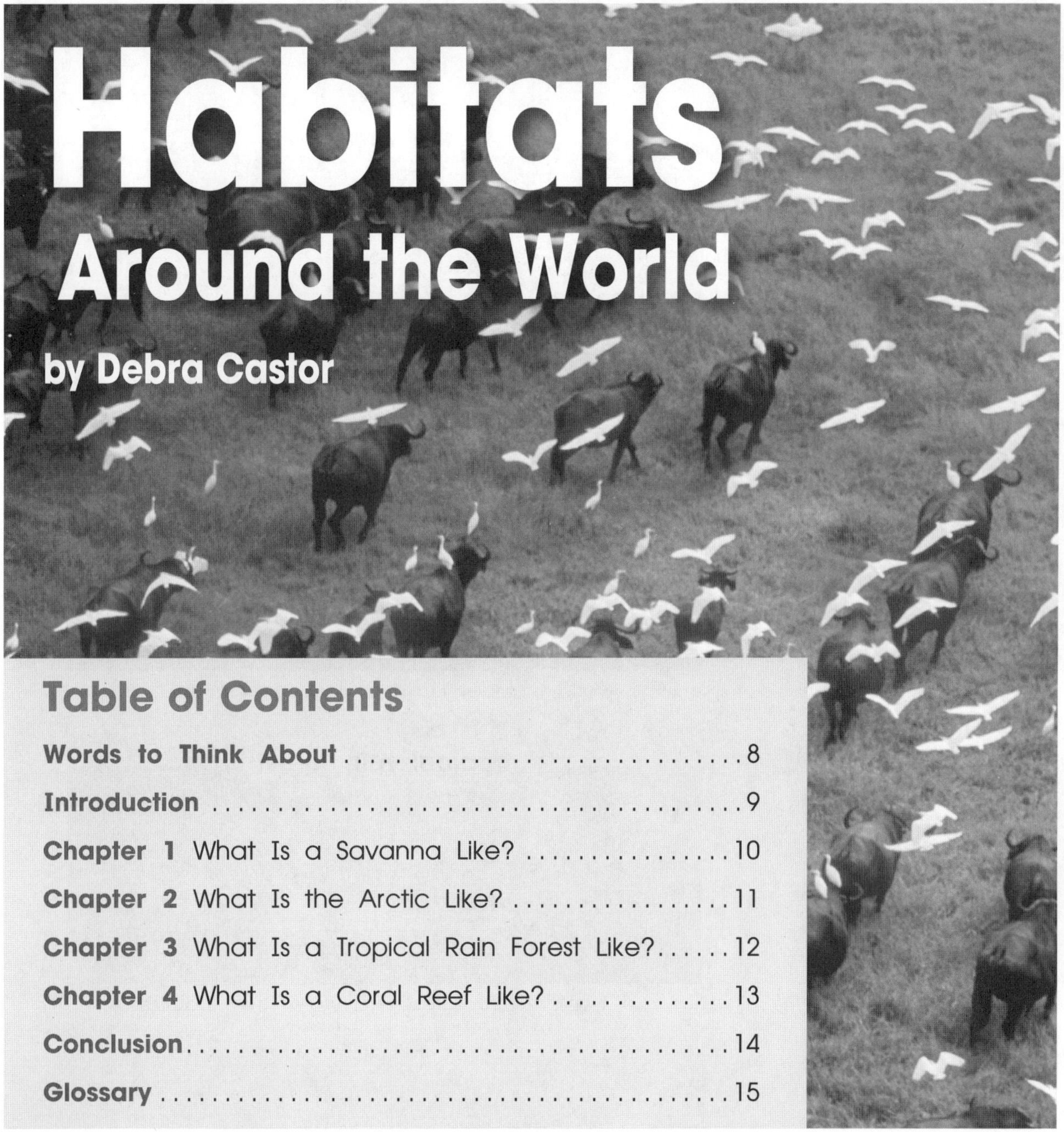

# Habitats
## Around the World

by Debra Castor

## Table of Contents

| | |
|---|---|
| Words to Think About | 8 |
| Introduction | 9 |
| Chapter 1 What Is a Savanna Like? | 10 |
| Chapter 2 What Is the Arctic Like? | 11 |
| Chapter 3 What Is a Tropical Rain Forest Like? | 12 |
| Chapter 4 What Is a Coral Reef Like? | 13 |
| Conclusion | 14 |
| Glossary | 15 |

# Words to Think About

**coral reef**

A coral reef is a habitat that forms in some oceans.

**the Arctic**

The Arctic is a very cold, windy habitat.

**habitats**

Animals live in many habitats.

**the world**

The world includes Earth and everything on Earth.

**savanna**

A savanna is a dry grassland habitat.

**tropical rain forest**

A tropical rain forest is a warm, wet habitat.

# Introduction

Earth has many **habitats**, or places where plants and animals live. We see habitats all around **the world**.

This book has four chapters. Each chapter is about a different habitat. As we read, try to imagine yourself in each place.

zebra

Arctic fox

orangutan

angelfish

Chapter 1

# What Is a Savanna Like?

A **savanna** is a grassland habitat. The weather is hot all year. The savanna has a long dry season when very little rain falls. Grasses grow quickly during the rainy season.

▲ Can you find the savannas on this map?

savannas

lion

acacia tree    elephants

giraffe

▲ Wildebeests migrate, or move, during the dry season.

**Closer to Home**

A prairie is another type of grassland. Canada and the United States of America have prairies.

© Benchmark Education Company, LLC

# Chapter 2

# What Is the Arctic Like?

**The Arctic** is a cold, windy polar habitat in the northern part of the world. The temperature in this habitat can be as cold as –30°F (–34°C).

The Arctic is so cold that the ground is frozen in many places.

▲ Find the Arctic on the map.

the Arctic

▲ Some people live in the Arctic. Could you?

harp seal

purple saxifrage

musk ox

Chapter 3

# What Is a Tropical Rain Forest Like?

A **tropical rain forest** is a very warm, very wet habitat near the equator. Imagine a big rain storm. Big storms have about four inches (ten centimeters) of rain.

A tropical rain forest can get 400 inches (1,000 centimeters) of rain each year!

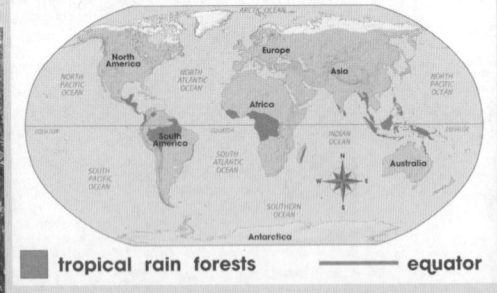

■ tropical rain forests ——— equator

▲ What continents have tropical rain forests?

▲ This tropical rain forest is in Australia.

macaw parrot

spider monkey

jaguar

**LOOK AT TEXT STRUCTURE**

**Description**

The author uses the words "wet" and "warm" to help readers understand what a tropical rain forest is like. What other words help you picture the habitats in this book?

12

© Benchmark Education Company, LLC

# Chapter 4

## What Is a Coral Reef Like?

A **coral reef** is a habitat in warm, shallow ocean water. A coral reef has millions of tiny coral polyps. The coral polyps are animals.

Polluting the water can hurt coral reefs. We can all protect this unique and colorful habitat.

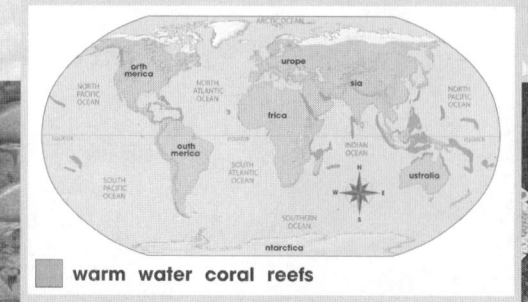

warm water coral reefs

▲ Find the coral reefs on this map.

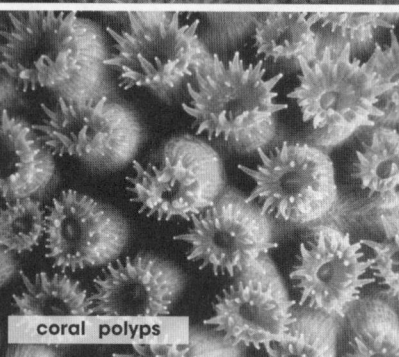

▲ People can use plants from coral reefs to make medicines.

angelfish

coral polyps

sea turtle

# Conclusion

Habitats are places where plants and animals live. Savannas, the Arctic, tropical rain forests, and coral reefs are four of Earth's many habitats.

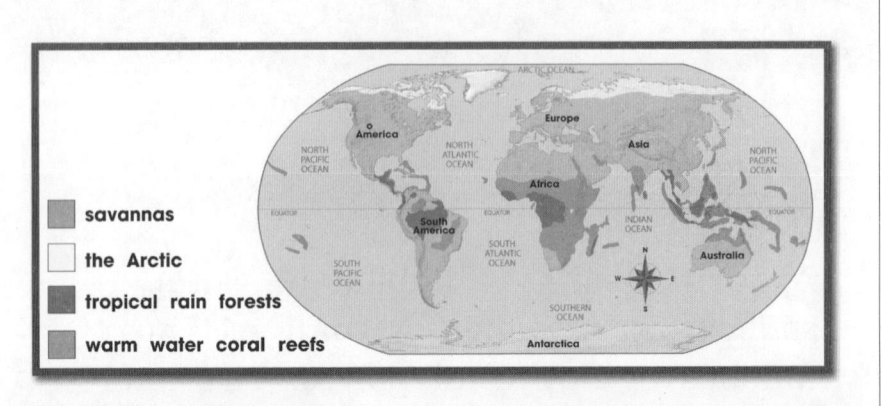

- savannas
- the Arctic
- tropical rain forests
- warm water coral reefs

**Savanna**
- grassland
- hot
- dry season
- rainy season

**Tropical Rain Forest**
- warm
- wet
- near equator

**The Arctic**
- cold
- windy
- frozen ground most of the year

**Coral Reef**
- forms in warm, shallow water

# Glossary

**coral reef** a habitat that is in warm, shallow ocean water

**habitats** places where plants and animals live

**savanna** a habitat with grass and some trees

**the Arctic** a cold habitat in the northern part of the world

**the world** Earth and all the living and nonliving things on Earth

**tropical rain forest** a hot, rainy habitat with many plants and animals

# Things I Like to Do

**Speaker 1:** I like to go for long walks with my dog.

**Speaker 2:** I like to run in the yard with my dog.

**Speaker 1:** I like to play board games that take all afternoon.

**Speaker 2:** I like to play computer games with lots of action. Wham! Zam!

**Speaker 1:** I like to bake cookies with my granddad.

**Speaker 2:** I like to grab a quick burger with my big brother.

**Speaker 1:** I like to learn new words. Today I learned to say au-to-bi-o-gra-phy.

**Speaker 2:** I like words, too. Did you know that some people say "soda" and some people say "pop"?

**Speaker 1 and Speaker 2:**
Y...a...w...n.
I like to take a nap.
See you later!

# Unit 2

## Table of Contents

As Good As New! . . . . . . . . . . . . .18

A Very Rare Cow . . . . . . . . . . . . .19

The Ants and Their Plants . . . . . . . .20

The Three Billy Goats Gruff . . . . . . .21

Snow . . . . . . . . . . . . . . . . . . .34

# As Good As New!

Brad liked to fix broken things. He fixed broken bikes and old clocks.

He fixed broken radios and computers, too.

Brad's grandma gave him a watch for his birthday.

"Thanks," said Brad. "I can't wait until this watch gets old."

"Why do you want it to get old?" asked his grandma.

"So it will break," said Brad. "Then I can make it like new again!"

# A Very Rare Cow

Mr. Phillips took his class to visit a rare animals farm.

"Look there," said Ian. "A flying pig!"

"Look over here!" shouted Mary. "A woodchuck chucking wood."

"Oh no," said Sylvia. "A crying cow."

The whole class turned to look at the very sad purple cow.

"What's wrong?" Sylvia asked. "How can we help?"

"I can't give milk," cried the purple cow. "I try and try, but all I have is purple grape juice."

"We love purple grape juice," said the students.

The purple cow stopped crying and walked proudly to the barn.

# The Ants and Their Plants

Ned and Ted Ant said, "We got more plants. We will eat all winter long."

Ron and Jon Ant said, "We played bug tug. We had fun!"

"All you do is play, play, play," said Ned and Ted. "What will you eat this winter?"

Winter came. Ron and Jon had no plants to eat. They went to Ned and Ted, and said, "We are sad. We have no more plants."

"You may eat some of our plants," said Ned. "But you must help next time

# The Three Billy Goats Gruff

retold by Brenda Parkes and Judith Smith • illustrated by Steve Harpster

Once upon a time
there were three Billy Goats Gruff.
There was a little Billy Goat Gruff,
and a middle-sized Billy Goat Gruff,
and a great big Billy Goat Gruff.

The three Billy Goats Gruff
lived on a hillside,
but they did not have enough to eat.
Over the bridge on another hill,
the grass was green and sweet.
But under the bridge lived
a bad-tempered Troll.

The Troll would not let the goats cross the bridge.
The three Billy Goats Gruff grew **hungrier** and **HUNGRIER**.
One day they were **so** hungry they decided
to cross the bridge.

Little Billy Goat Gruff went first,
**Trip trap trip trap**
over the bridge.
**"WHO'S THAT CROSSING OVER MY BRIDGE?"**
said the Troll.

" 'Tis only I, the littlest Billy Goat Gruff," called the first Billy Goat Gruff.

**"I'M GOING TO COME AND EAT YOU UP!"** roared the Troll.

"OH! Please don't eat me. Wait for my brother, the middle-sized Billy Goat Gruff. He's much bigger than I am," replied Little Billy Goat Gruff.

"Oh! Very well!
**Then be off with you,"**
said the Troll.

The little Billy Goat ran away
and ate the sweet green grass.

Middle-sized Billy Goat Gruff went next,
**Trip trap trip trap** over the bridge.

**"WHO'S THAT CROSSING OVER MY BRIDGE?"** said the Troll.

" 'Tis only I, the middle-sized Billy Goat Gruff," called the second Billy Goat Gruff.

**"I'M GOING TO COME AND EAT YOU UP!"** roared the Troll.

"OH! Please don't eat me. Wait for my brother, Great Big Billy Goat Gruff. He's much bigger than I am," replied Middle-sized Billy Goat Gruff.

"Oh! Very well!
**Then be off with you,**"
said the Troll.

The middle-sized
Billy Goat Gruff
ran away and ate
the sweet green grass.

Then Great Big Billy Goat Gruff began to cross the bridge.
He was big and mean and **hungry**.
**Trip trap trip trap**
over the bridge.

"WHO'S THAT CROSSING OVER MY BRIDGE?"
said the Troll.

" 'Tis I, Great Big Billy Goat Gruff," shouted the third Billy Goat Gruff.

"I'M GOING TO COME AND EAT YOU UP!" roared the Troll.

He climbed up on to the bridge.

The great big Billy Goat
stopped still.
DOWN went his horns,
and he rushed at the Troll.
He butted him once
**twice**
**three** times.

The Troll tumbled off
the bridge,

**down**

**down**

down

into the deep water
under the bridge.

The great big Billy Goat went
**Trip trap trip trap**
over the bridge and up the hill.

Soon he was eating the sweet green grass.

The three Billy Goats Gruff lived happily ever after. They always had plenty to eat, and no one has ever seen the Troll again.

## What happened in the story?

33

# Snow

Many people like snow.

Kids like to go sledding, build a snowman, and throw snowballs.

People take lots of pictures because the trees look so pretty.

People can ski on the fresh snow, called powder.

Snowplow drivers have to work hard, but they feel good helping people.

Some people don't like snow, though.

Snow makes things harder for mail carriers, farmers, builders, and pilots.

Do you like snow?

# Unit 3

## Table of Contents

Making Pizza . . . . . . . . . . . . . . .36

Pickled Pepper Stew . . . . . . . . . . .37

Ducklings Grow Up . . . . . . . . . . . .38

The Life Cycle of a Butterfly . . . . . . .39

Knock-Knock Jokes . . . . . . . . . . . .48

# Making Pizza

It's fun to watch the pizza man work. First, he tosses a lump of dough high in the air. He keeps tossing until the dough is flat and round. Next, he puts the dough on a tray. Then, he adds sauce, cheese, and toppings. He's almost done! The pizza goes into the oven until it is hot and crispy. Finally, it's time to eat!

# Pickled Pepper Stew

Peter Piper had a pepper farm. He picked green peppers. Then he picked red peppers. Peter Piper picked yellow peppers, too! Most of all, Peter Piper loved pickled pepper stew.

In went some red peppers. Next, the green peppers flew. Finally, a yellow pepper dove right into the stew.

I wouldn't dive into pickled pepper stew, would you?

© Benchmark Education Company, LLC

# Ducklings Grow Up

Ducklings grow up fast! First a mother duck lays some eggs. Then little ducklings hatch from the eggs. Soon the ducklings are sleeping and eating. They are walking, too.

Next, the ducklings are swimming with their mother. The ducklings get bigger and bigger. Finally, the ducklings grow to become ducks!

# The Life Cycle of a Butterfly

by Margaret McNamara

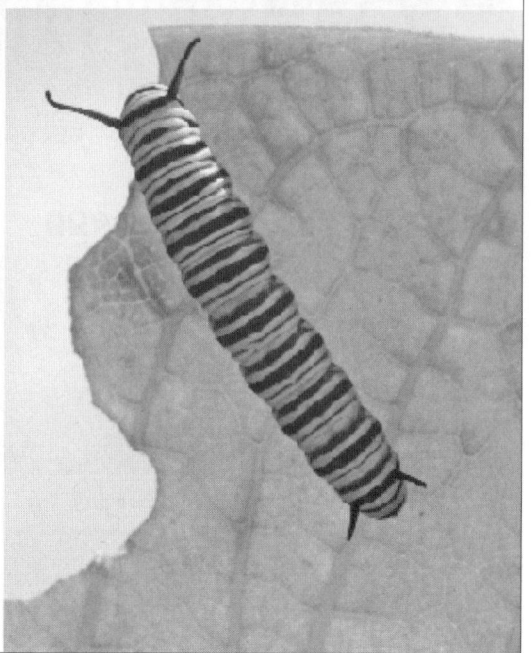

## Table of Contents

| | |
|---|---|
| Words to Think About | 40 |
| Introduction | 41 |
| **Chapter 1** How Does a Butterfly Begin? | 42 |
| **Chapter 2** How Does a Butterfly Grow? | 43 |
| **Chapter 3** What Does an Adult Butterfly Do? | 45 |
| Conclusion | 46 |
| Glossary | 47 |

© Benchmark Education Company, LLC

# Words to Think About

**butterfly**

A butterfly is an insect.

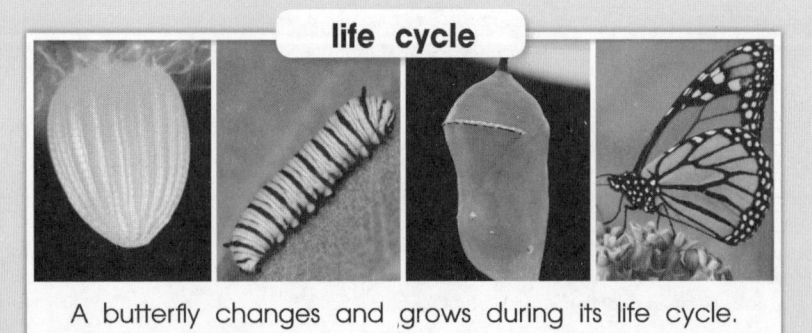

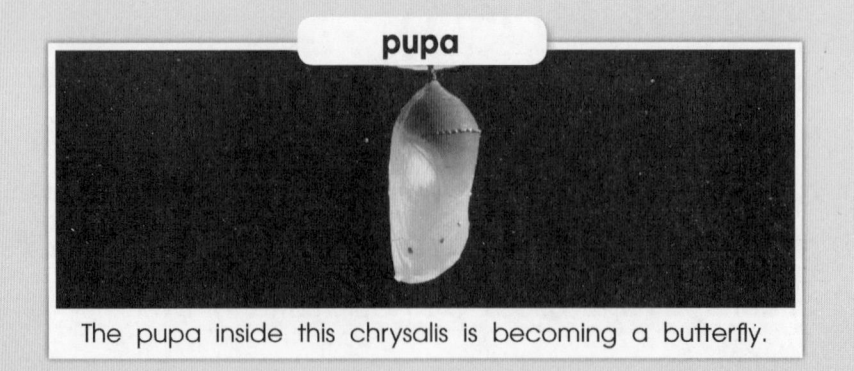

**larva**

A larva hatches from an egg.

**caterpillar**

This caterpillar will become a butterfly.

**life cycle**

A butterfly changes and grows during its life cycle.

**egg**

A butterfly begins life as an egg.

**pupa**

The pupa inside this chrysalis is becoming a butterfly.

# Introduction

All animals have a **life cycle**. First, animals begin life.

Then animals grow and change. Finally, animals die.

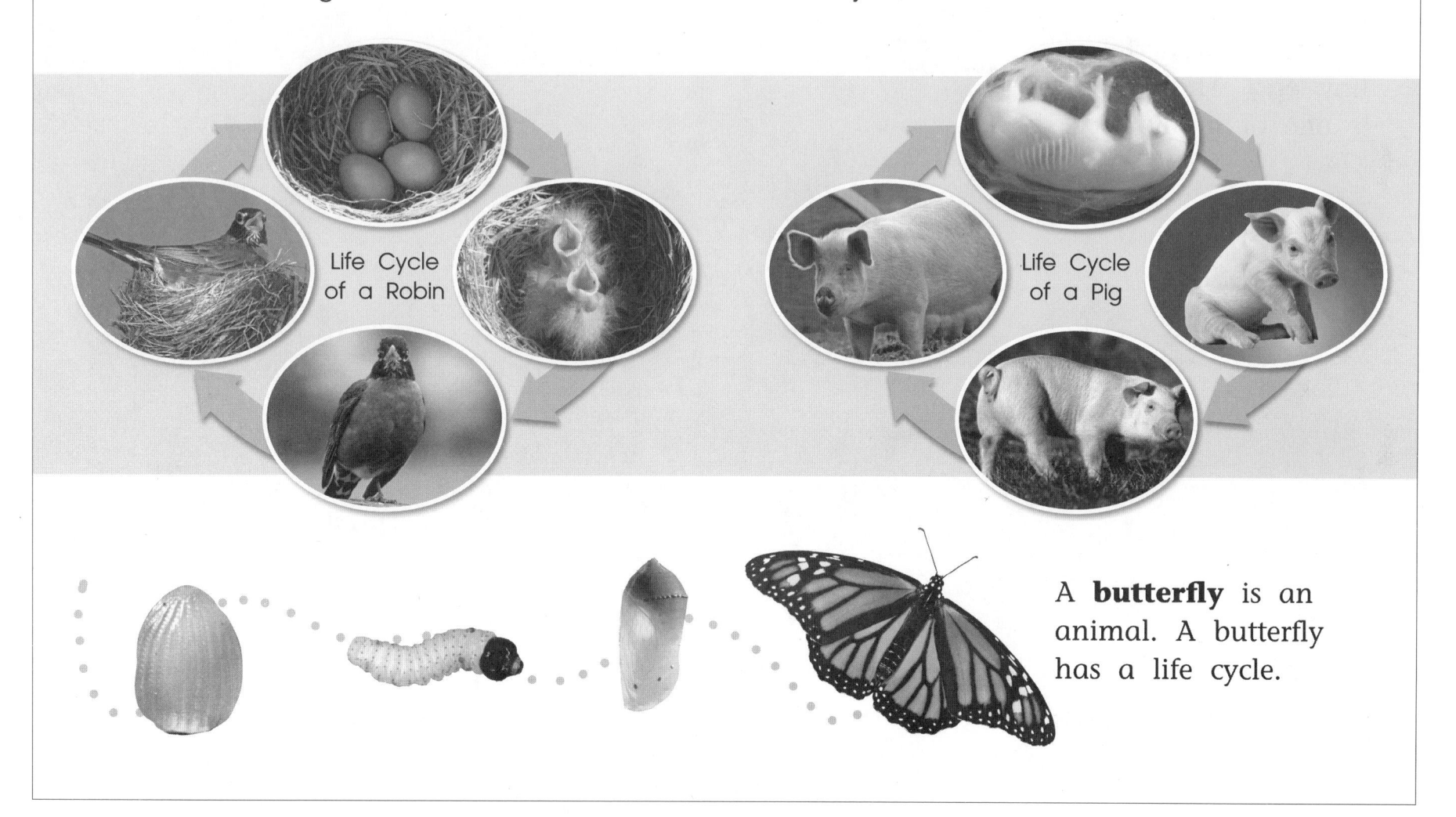

Life Cycle of a Robin

Life Cycle of a Pig

A **butterfly** is an animal. A butterfly has a life cycle.

**Chapter 1**

# How Does a Butterfly Begin?

At first, a butterfly is a tiny **egg**. The tiny egg is one of many eggs.

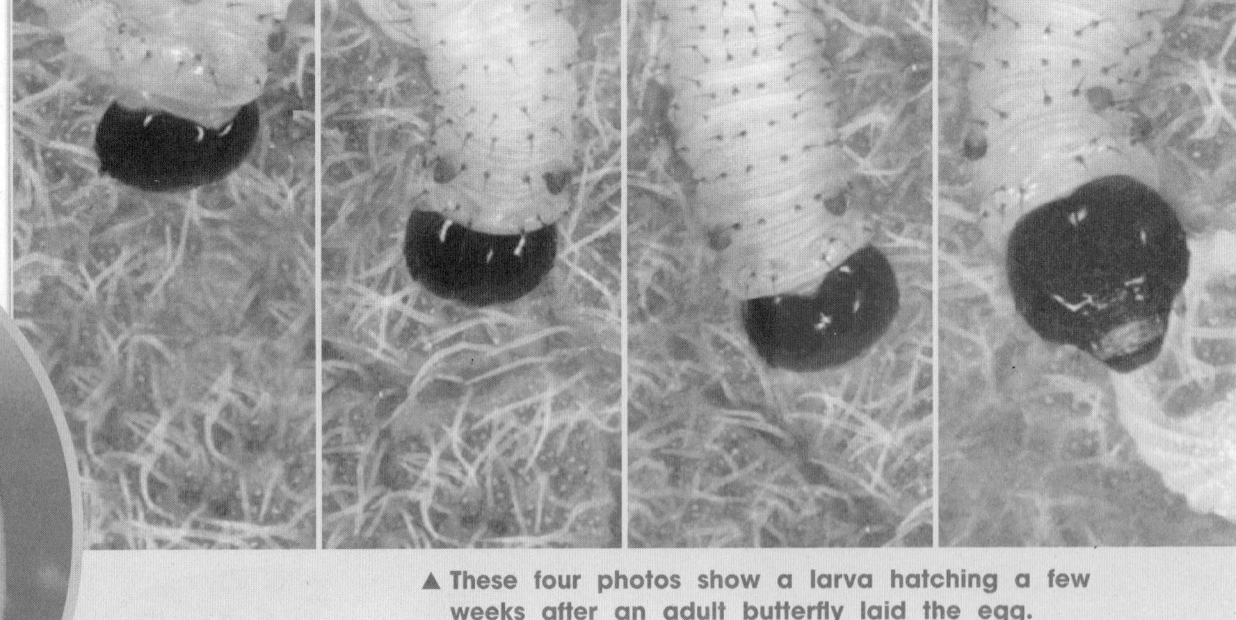

▲ These four photos show a larva hatching a few weeks after an adult butterfly laid the egg.

◄ An adult butterfly laid this egg on a leaf.

Next, a **larva** hatches from the egg. The larva is a **caterpillar**.

© Benchmark Education Company, LLC

Chapter 2

# How Does a Butterfly Grow?

The caterpillar grows very quickly. The caterpillar grows quickly because it eats a large amount of food.

A caterpillar spends almost all of its time searching for food. ▶

Then the caterpillar attaches to a leaf or a twig.

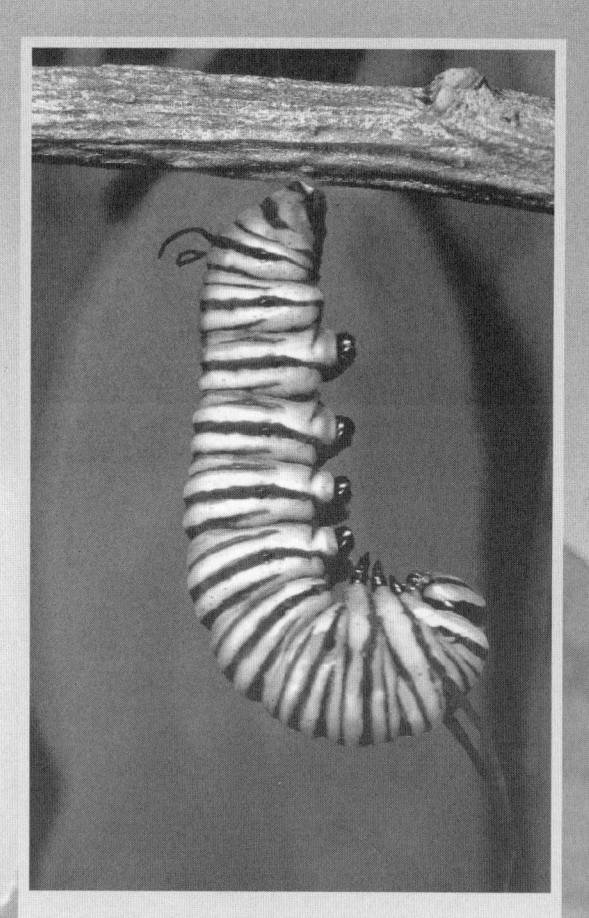

▲ This caterpillar will soon change form.

Chapter 2

How Does a Butterfly Grow?

After attaching to the twig, the caterpillar sheds its skin for the last time. Then the caterpillar grows a hard shell.

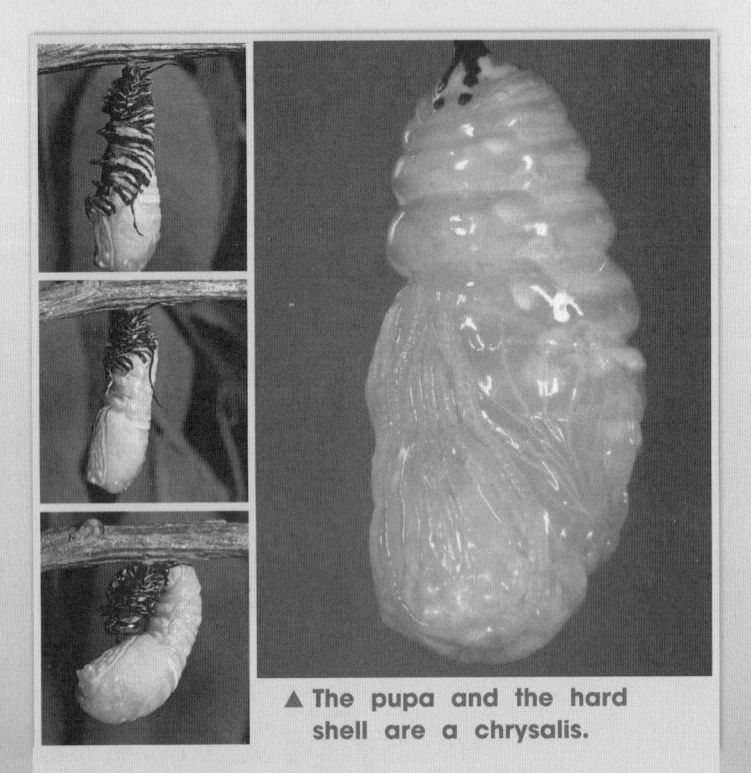

Inside the shell is a **pupa**. The pupa becomes an adult butterfly.

▲ The pupa and the hard shell are a chrysalis.

LOOK AT TEXT STRUCTURE

**Sequence of Events**

Notice the words "After attaching to the twig." These words tell you about the sequence, or order, of events in the life cycle. What other word on this page helps you understand the sequence of events?

▲ A butterfly crawls out of the hard shell.

© Benchmark Education Company, LLC

**Chapter 3**

# What Does an Adult Butterfly Do?

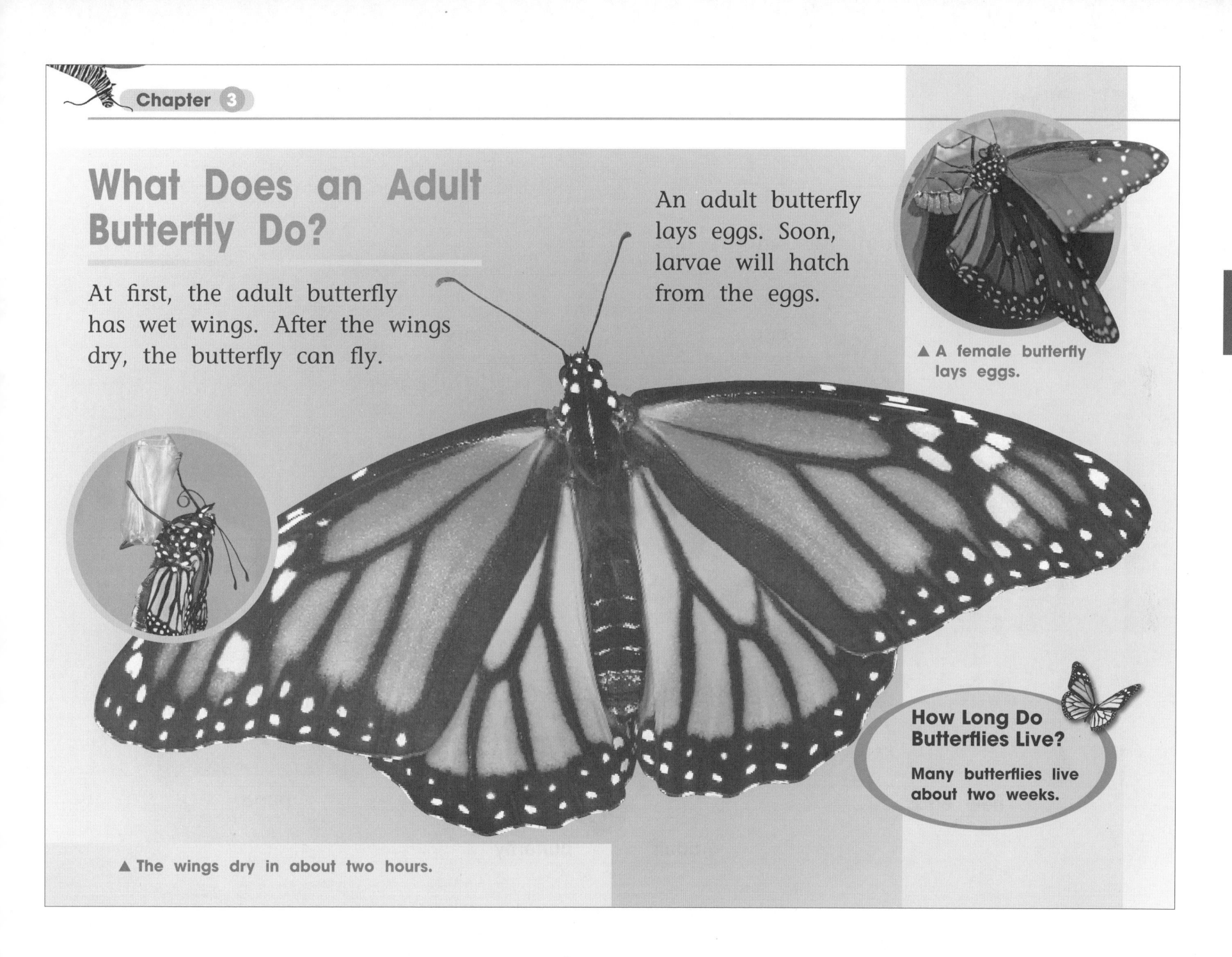

At first, the adult butterfly has wet wings. After the wings dry, the butterfly can fly.

An adult butterfly lays eggs. Soon, larvae will hatch from the eggs.

▲ A female butterfly lays eggs.

**How Long Do Butterflies Live?**

Many butterflies live about two weeks.

▲ The wings dry in about two hours.

## Conclusion

A butterfly is an animal. A butterfly has a life cycle.

egg

larva

new eggs

adult butterfly

pupa

# Glossary

**butterfly** an insect with wings

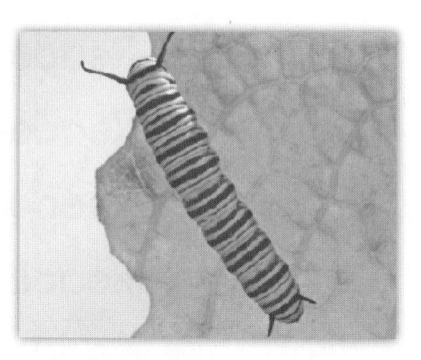

**caterpillar** the larva of a butterfly

**egg** the first stage of life for many animals

**larva** the second stage of life for some insects

**life cycle** the order of how a living thing changes as it grows

**pupa** a butterfly just before it grows wings

# Knock-Knock Jokes

**Reader 1:** Knock, knock.
**Reader 2:** Who's there?
**Reader 1:** Ben.
**Reader 2:** Ben who?
**Reader 1:** Ben knocking on the door all afternoon!

**Reader 1:** Knock, knock.
**Reader 2:** Who's there?
**Reader 1:** Isadore.
**Reader 2:** Isadore who?
**Reader 1:** Isadore made out of wood?

**Reader 1:** Knock, knock.
**Reader 2:** Who's there?
**Reader 1:** Norma Lee.
**Reader 2:** Norma Lee who?
**Reader 1:** Norma Lee I'd use the doorbell, but it's broken!

# Unit 4

## Table of Contents

The Crow and the Pitcher . . . . . . . . .50

Three Eggs . . . . . . . . . . . . . .51

Sandy Squirrel . . . . . . . . . . . . .52

The Little Red Hen . . . . . . . . .53

Student Interview . . . . . . . . . . . . .62

© Benchmark Education Company, LLC

# The Crow and the Pitcher

A thirsty crow was in a garden. He saw a pitcher half full of water. He could not reach the water with his beak. He tried to knock the pitcher over, but he could not. Then he had an idea.

One by one, he dropped stones in the pitcher. The water rose. Finally, he could reach the water with his beak! He was no longer thirsty.

# Three Eggs

Ms. Trent brought a box to school. The girls and boys looked inside the box. They saw three eggs.

"What's inside the eggs?" asked the boys and girls.

Ms. Trent said, "Soon the eggs will hatch. Then we will find out." A few days passed. The eggs hatched. Out came three baby chicks.

# Sandy Squirrel

Sandy Squirrel looks across the deep, blue water. She sees a patch of ripe berries on the other side.

"How can I get there?" she wonders. "I can't swim."

Just then, Tommy Turtle pokes his head out of the water.

"Hop on my back," says Tommy. "I'll take you to the other side." Sandy thanks Tommy. Then she hops on his back and off they go.

# The Little Red Hen

retold by Brenda Parkes and Judith Smith
illustrated by James Palmer

One spring morning,
the little Red Hen
found a grain of wheat.
She asked the duck,
"Will you help me plant
this grain of wheat?"
"**Not I**," quacked the duck.
"I've got better things to do."

She asked the dog,
"Will you help me plant
this grain of wheat?"
"**Not I**," barked the dog.
"I've got better things to do."

She asked the cat,
"Will you help me plant
this grain of wheat?"
"**Not I**," meowed the cat.
"I've got better
things to do."

She asked the pig,
"Will you help me plant
this grain of wheat?"
"**Not I**," grunted the pig.
"I've got better things to do."

"Then I'll plant it myself," said the little Red Hen. And she did.

The wheat grew tall and it ripened. "Who will help me cut the wheat?" asked the little Red Hen.

"**Not I**," quacked the duck.
"**Not I**," barked the dog.
"**Not I**," meowed the cat.
"**Not I**," grunted the pig.

Then I will do it myself,"
said the little Red Hen.
And she did.

Now the wheat was ready
to go to the mill.
"Who will help me take
the wheat to the mill?"
asked the little Red Hen.

GRAIN MILL

"**Not I**," quacked the duck.
"**Not I**," barked the dog.
"**Not I**," meowed the cat.
"**Not I**," grunted the pig.

"Then I will do it myself,"
said the little Red Hen.
And she did.

When she got home with the flour
she asked,
"Who will help me make the bread?"

"**Not I**," quacked the duck.
"**Not I**," barked the dog.
"**Not I**," meowed the cat.
"**Not I**," grunted the pig.

"Then I will make it myself," said the little Red Hen. And she did.

Soon the bread was ready to bake. "Who will help me bake the bread?" asked the little Red Hen.

"**Not I**," quacked the duck.
"**Not I**," barked the dog.
"**Not I**," meowed the cat.
"**Not I**," grunted the pig.

"Then I will do it myself," said the little Red Hen. And she did.

When the bread was cooked she took it out of the oven. She put it on the table to cool.

When the bread was cool she asked, "Who will help me eat the bread?"

"**I will!**" quacked the duck.
"**I will!**" barked the dog.
"**I will!**" meowed the cat.
"**I will!**" grunted the pig.

"**Oh, no, you won't!**"
said the little Red Hen.
"I will eat it myself."

**And she did!**

## What happened in the story?

# Student Interview

**Teacher:** What's your favorite animal?

**Student:** I like my dog. He's a Chocolate Lab named Brownie.

**Teacher:** What's your favorite pair of shoes?

**Student:** I like my brown shoes. They're the color of chocolate.

**Teacher:** What's your favorite part of school?

**Student:** I like lunchtime. Sometimes my mom packs a chocolate bar in my lunch box.

**Teacher:** I think I know the answer to the next question. What's your favorite flavor of ice cream?

**Student:** I like vanilla. Surprise!

# Unit 5

## Table of Contents

A Merry Old Soul . . . . . . . . . . . . . .64

Animals in Winter . . . . . . . . . . . .65

Plus None! . . . . . . . . . . . . . . . . .66

Life in a Suburban Community . . . . .67

The Hungry Fox. . . . . . . . . . . . . .76

# A Merry Old Soul

In the middle of the night, Old King Cole woke up and could not fall back to sleep.

He called for his pipe. Old King Cole called for his fiddlers three.

"Play a song for me," said Old King Cole. "I like the song that goes 'Tweedle dee, tweedle dee.'"

# Animals in Winter

What do some animals do in winter? Some animals go underground. Some animals go into caves. These animals stay inside and sleep until spring.

Some animals find a new home in winter. Many birds fly to warmer places where they can find food.

# Plus None!

I can add! One basket has 5 apples. The other basket has 0 apples. There are 5 apples in all.

One basket has 0 toys. The other basket has 7 toys. There are 7 toys in all.

# Life in a Suburban Community

by Margaret McNamara

## Table of Contents

Words to Think About . . . . . . . . . . . . . . . . . .68

Introduction . . . . . . . . . . . . . . . . . . . . . . . . . .69

**Chapter 1** Homes . . . . . . . . . . . . . . . . . . . . . .70

**Chapter 2** Jobs . . . . . . . . . . . . . . . . . . . . . . . .71

**Chapter 3** Places to Play . . . . . . . . . . . . . .73

Conclusion . . . . . . . . . . . . . . . . . . . . . . . . . . .74

Glossary . . . . . . . . . . . . . . . . . . . . . . . . . . . . .75

© Benchmark Education Company, LLC

# Words to Think About

**community helpers** 
These community helpers work for the community.

**jobs** 
People have jobs so they can earn money.

**commute** 
Many people commute, or travel, to work in the city.

**neighborhood** 
This neighborhood is in a suburban community.

**homes** 
People live in many types of homes.

**suburban community** 
People live, work, and play in this suburban community.

# Introduction

A community is a place where people live, work, and play. Many people live in **suburban communities**.

A suburban community is near a big city.

▲ This neighborhood is in a suburban community.

**Other Types of Communities**

urban community

rural community

# Chapter 1

# Homes

In a suburban community, many families live in houses. Families in suburbs live in townhouses and mobile **homes**, too.

Most people have more living space than people in big cities. Many people have yards and garages.

▲ Families live in these houses.

mobile homes

townhouses

**Chapter 2**

# Jobs

Did you know that some people who live in a suburb work in a nearby city? In the morning, they **commute** to their **jobs**, and at night they return home.

Other people work right in their **neighborhood**. For example, every suburban community has teachers, doctors, and nurses.

**LOOK AT TEXT STRUCTURE**

**Description**

The author uses the words "for example" to describe, or give information about, jobs in a suburban community.

▲ These people commute to work in the big city.

doctors

teacher

© Benchmark Education Company, LLC

Chapter 2　　　　　　　　　　　　　　　　　　　　　　　　　　　　　Jobs

Some people are **community helpers**. Every suburban community needs firefighters, police officers, mail carriers, and garbage collectors.

Other people work in stores. They know many people in the community.

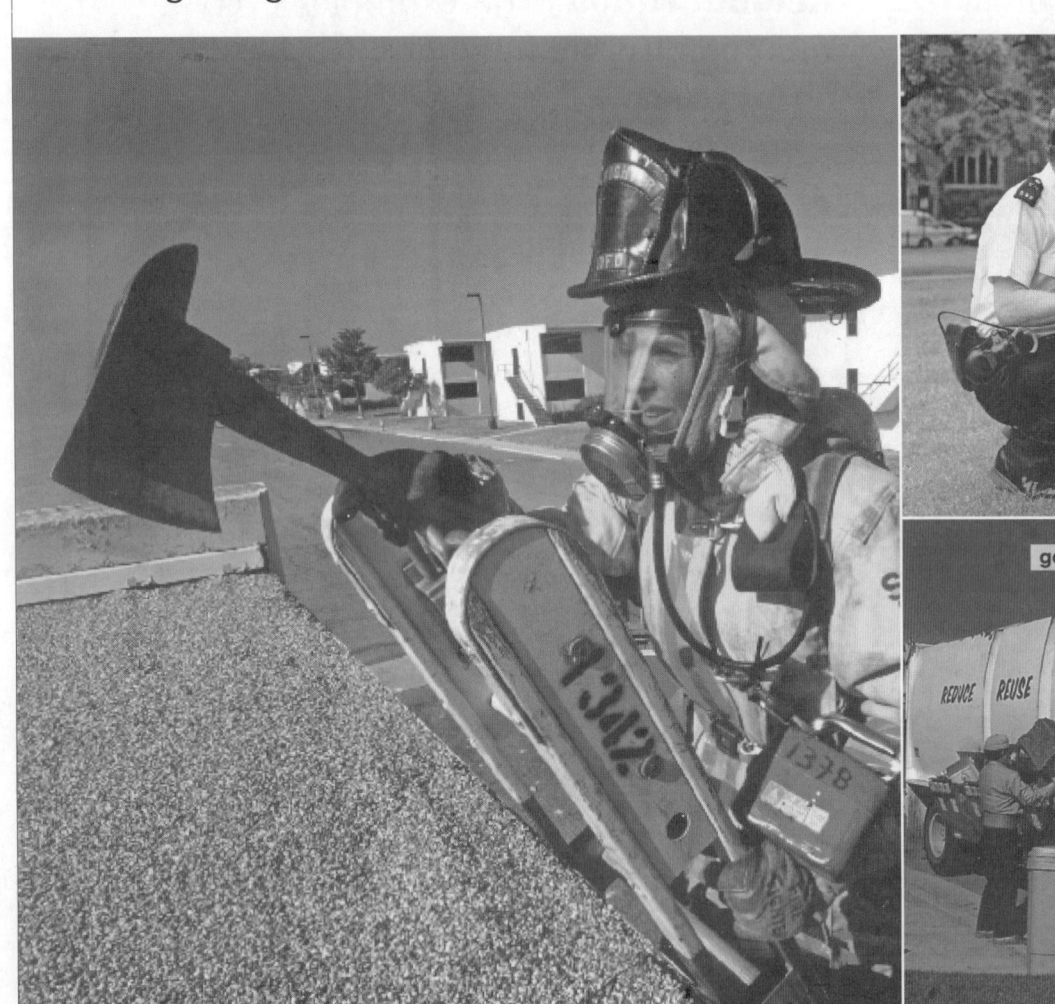

pharmacist

police officer

mail carrier

garbage collector

### Going Green

Does your community recycle? If not, be a community helper! Collect old newspapers, empty cans, and empty bottles. Then take the items to a recycling center.

# Chapter 3

## Places to Play

You don't have to go very far in a suburban community to find a place to play. Many people have backyards where children can play.

Some neighborhoods have pools. They have parks and playgrounds, too.

public pool

skating rink

▲ Many people play in their own backyards.

## Conclusion

Many families live in suburban communities. Suburbs are near big cities.

### Suburban Community

| homes | jobs | places to play |

# Glossary

**community helpers** people who have jobs that help the community

**commute** to travel back and forth regularly

**homes** places where people live

**jobs** types of work that people do

**neighborhood** part of a community

**suburban community** a place near a big city where people live, work, and play

# The Hungry Fox

Fox went to the farm. He wanted to eat Rooster.

Cow got up. "Shoo, Fox, shoo!" said Cow. "Go away! Come back some other day."

Sheep got up. "Shoo, Fox, shoo!" said Sheep. "Go away! Come back some other day."

Pig got up. "Shoo, Fox, shoo!" said Pig. "Go away! Come back some other day."

Rooster got up. "Cock-a-doodle-doo!" said Rooster.

The farmer got up. "Shoo, Fox, shoo!" said the farmer. "Go away, and do NOT come back some other day!"

# Unit 6

## Table of Contents

Cat Care . . . . . . . . . . . . . . . . .78

Water . . . . . . . . . . . . . . . . . . .79

Our Money . . . . . . . . . . . . . . .80

Needs Past and Present . . . . . . . . .81

Tiny Tim . . . . . . . . . . . . . . . . .90

# Cat Care

Cats are fun pets. Cats need care to stay happy and healthy. Cats need fresh water and food every day. Playing is good exercise for cats. Cats like to chase balls and play with toys. Don't forget to give your cat lots of love, too.

# Water

Water is everywhere.
We see water at the beach.
We use water to play.
A water fountain has water.
We use water to drink.
We find water in the bathroom.

We use water to wash our hands.
Water is in the kitchen. We use water to cook. We see water outside. We use water in the garden.

# Our Money

We use money every day. We use money to buy things for school. The food we eat costs money. We use money when we go to a movie.

Things cost different amounts of money. A movie might cost $10. Lunch might cost $3. A book might cost $4. We should try not to spend all of our money. We should save some.

# Needs Past and Present

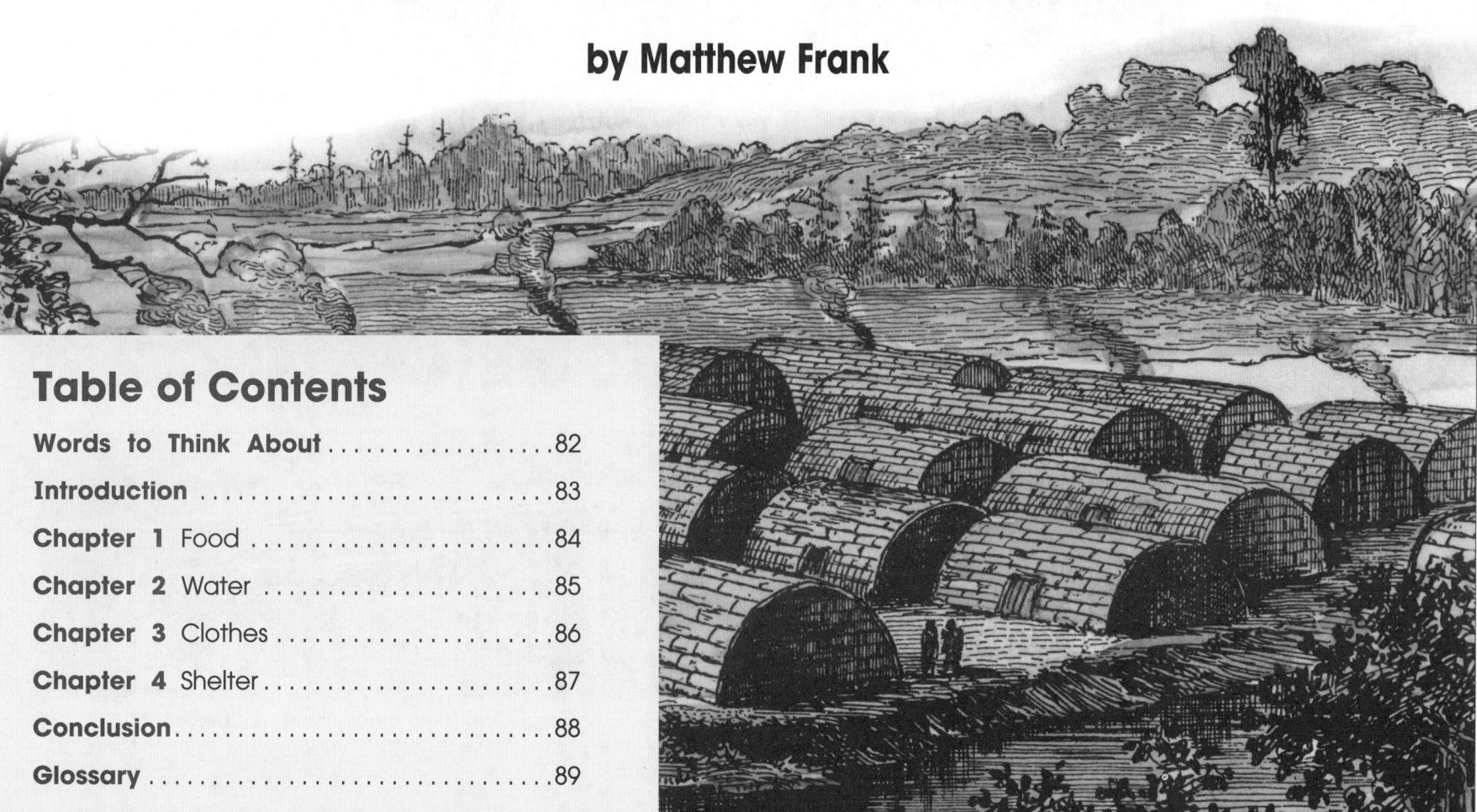

by Matthew Frank

## Table of Contents

**Words to Think About** ................. 82

**Introduction** ........................... 83

**Chapter 1** Food ........................ 84

**Chapter 2** Water ....................... 85

**Chapter 3** Clothes ..................... 86

**Chapter 4** Shelter ..................... 87

**Conclusion** ............................ 88

**Glossary** .............................. 89

© Benchmark Education Company, LLC

# Words to Think About

**crops**

People grow these crops for food.

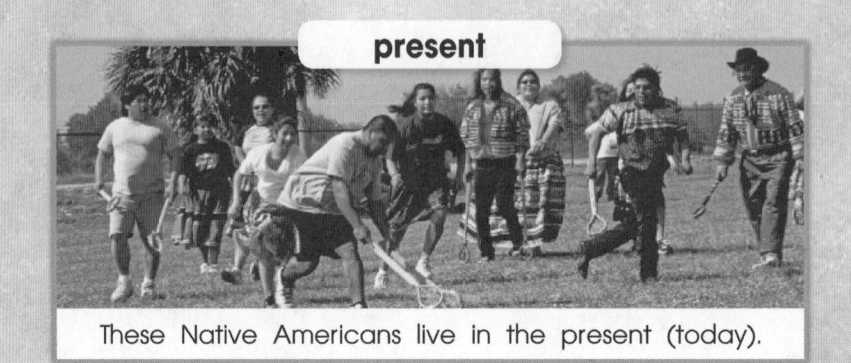

**Native Americans**

Native Americans were the first Americans.

**past**

These Native Americans lived in the past (long ago).

**present**

These Native Americans live in the present (today).

**shelter**

People had homes for shelter.

**stores**

Today we buy many things in stores.

# Introduction

You need food, water, and clothing. You also need a place to live. People in the **past** had these needs, too.

Over time, the ways people meet their needs have changed. This book tells how. It compares people today with **Native Americans** long ago.

food

water

clothing

shelter

Chapter 1

# Food

People need food to live. In the past, Native Americans hunted, caught fish, and grew **crops**.

In the **present**, people eat many of the same foods that the Native Americans ate. But most people buy their food in **stores**.

▲ The Pueblo grew corn.

▲ Today most of the food we buy and eat is grown on large farms.

### Food for Thought

The first crop was squash. People still grow squash today.

hunting

crops

grocery store

© Benchmark Education Company, LLC

# Chapter 2

# Water

All living things need water. Long ago, many Native Americans got water from rivers and lakes.

Today most people have water in their homes. But the water still comes from rivers and lakes.

▲ These Native Americans used water to cook.

▲ Today people turn on a faucet to get water.

▲ Now many people buy water.

85

# Chapter 3

# Clothes

Clothes keep us warm and protect us from the hot sun. Long ago, Native Americans made their own clothes.

We wear clothes today, too. However, most of us buy our clothes in stores.

▲ Native Americans used materials they could make or find.

▲ Do you make your clothes, or do you shop for them?

**LOOK AT TEXT STRUCTURE**

**Compare and Contrast**
The author uses the word "however" to show a contrast between the past and the present.

**Chapter 4**

# Shelter

People need **shelter** to stay safe. Each Native American group built homes from materials where they lived.

Today builders make our homes. People live in apartments, houses, mobile homes, and houseboats.

▲ The Lakota used buffalo hides to make tepees.

▲ Homes are made of bricks, wood, and many other materials.

igloos

clay and straw adobe houses

houseboats

mobile homes

# Conclusion

Long ago, people needed food, water, clothing, and shelter.

Today we still have these needs, but we meet them in different ways. How might people meet these needs in the future?

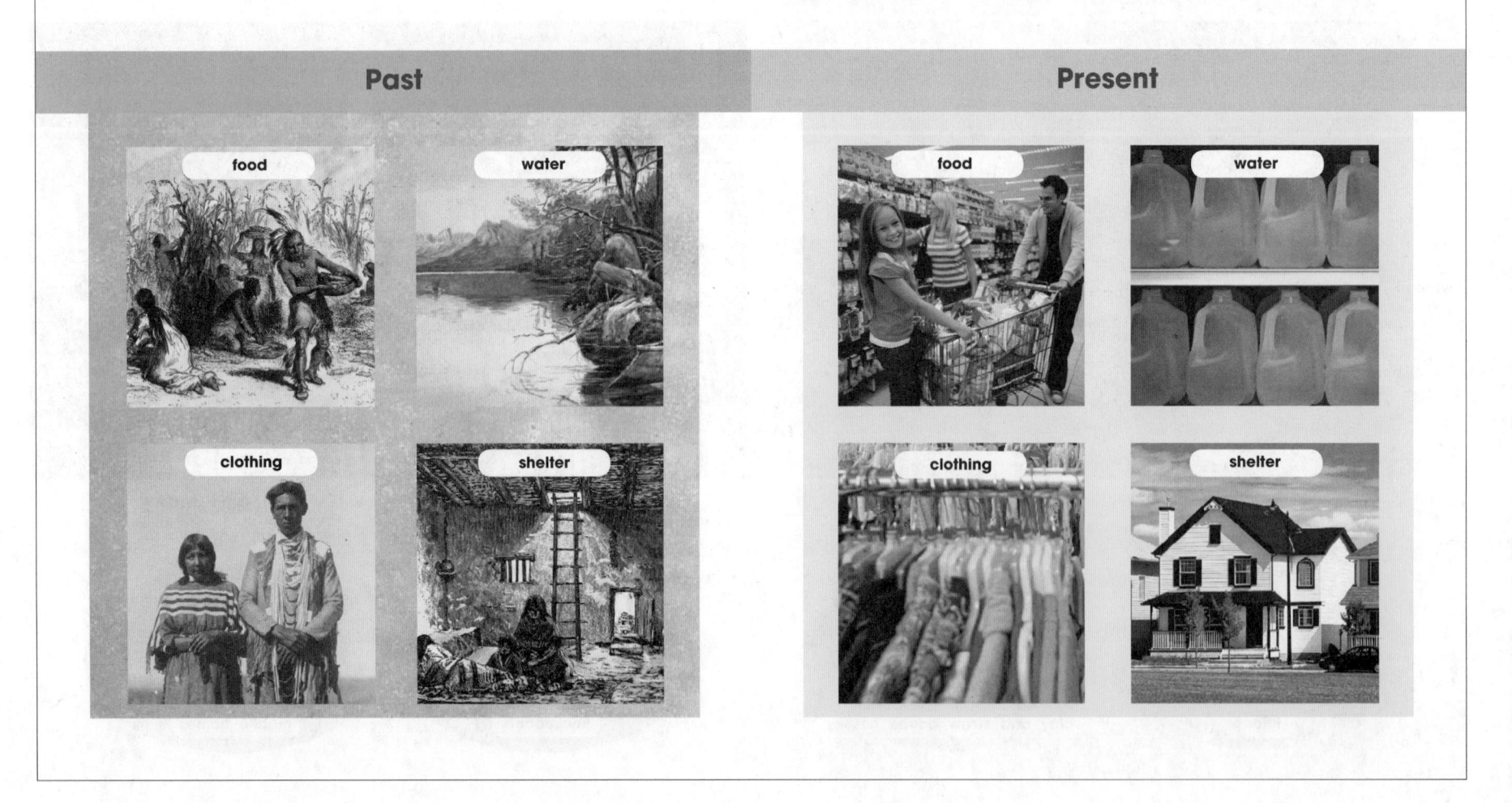

## Past

- food
- water
- clothing
- shelter

## Present

- food
- water
- clothing
- shelter

# Glossary

**crops** plants that people use

**Native Americans** the first people to live in America

**past** time that has already happened

**present** time that is happening now

**shelter** a safe place to live

**stores** places where people buy and sell things

# Tiny Tim

I had a little puppy.
His name was Tiny Tim.
I put him in the bathtub
To see if he could swim.

He drank up all the water.
He ate a bar of soap.
The next thing I knew,
He had a bubble in his throat.

In came the doctor,
In came the nurse,
In came the lady with the
alligator purse.

"Mumps!" said the doctor.
"Measles!" said the nurse.
"Hiccups!" said the lady with the
alligator purse.

Out went the doctor.
Out went the nurse.
Out went the lady with the
alligator purse.

# Unit 7

## Table of Contents

Can We Have a Pet? . . . . . . . . . . .92

Winter Weather Report . . . . . . . . . .93

A Life Cycle . . . . . . . . . . . . . . .94

The Three Shapely Pigs . . . . . . . . . .95

Bus Trip . . . . . . . . . . . . . . . . 104

# Can We Have a Pet?

Tim asked, "Can we have a pet?"

Mom said, "Yes, we can have a pet that doesn't have hair."

Tim asked, "Can we have a dog?"

Mom said, "Most dogs have hair. We cannot have a dog."

Tim asked, "Can we have a cat?"

Mom said, "Most cats have hair. We cannot have a cat."

Tim asked, "Can we have a fish?"

What do you think Mom said?

# Winter Weather Report

What will you do today?
What will you wear?
Look outside. Is the sun in the sky?
No. Clouds are in the sky. The clouds are dark. The clouds are low.
What will happen next?
Look at the thermometer. The temperature is very low.

# A Life Cycle

A tree drops a seed. Roots grow from the seed. The roots grow into the ground. A stem grows from the seed. Leaves grow from the stem. The plant grows and grows. What will the seed become?

# The Three Shapely Pigs

by Linda Johns • illustrated by John Bennett

These aren't the pigs you've met before.
These three pigs know so much more.

They make their plans with pencil and pen.
They don't give up 'til half past ten.

"I need a house,"
said the round little pig.
"Not too small,
but not too big."

The pigs worked together—
a team of three.
The round pig said,
"A house for me!"

"I need a house,"
said the square little pig.
"Not too small,
but not too big."

The pigs worked together—
just these two.
The house of squares
grew and grew!

"I need a house,"
said the last little pig.
"Not too small,
but not too big."

He worked all alone—
just this one.
And then at last
the job was done.

# Then a wolf came to town...

The wolf had her eye on the round little house. She crept to the door, quiet as a mouse.

She couldn't fit through
the round little door.
So she tried the square one
'til half past four.

She tried the last one
but did not fit.
"These shapes don't work—
not the least little bit."

The three little pigs saw
the wolf was tired.
"We have an idea—
and it's inspired!"

They took a circle,
a triangle, a square.
They put shapes together
with a great deal of care.

The wolf said, "Thanks!
This is right for me!"

If you built a house,
what shape would it be?

# What Is This Story About?

Use the pictures below to retell the story.

# Bus Trip

**Group 1:** Look for some people.
**Group 2:** How many people?
**Group 1:** A number of people.
**Group 2:** What will they do?
**Group 1:** Get on the bus.
**Group 2:** Could you go? You and I?

**Group 1:** We will go. Now is the time.
**Group 2:** We will go. From here to there.
**Group 1 and Group 2:** This is a good day!

# Unit 8

## Table of Contents

Butterflies and Moths . . . . . . . . . . 106

Monkeys and Apes . . . . . . . . . . . 107

Families . . . . . . . . . . . . . . . . . 108

Plants and the Seasons . . . . . . . . . 109

Treasure Island? . . . . . . . . . . . . 118

# Butterflies and Moths

Butterflies and moths are both flying insects. They like to eat the same green plants. However, there are differences between butterflies and moths. Most butterflies have colorful wings, while most moths do not have brightly colored wings.

# Monkeys and Apes

Monkeys and apes are alike in some ways. For example, both animals use fingers and thumbs to grab things. Monkeys and apes look alike, too.

Monkeys and apes are different in some ways. Apes are larger than monkeys, and apes don't have tails. Most monkeys live in trees. Apes live on the ground. Apes are good at climbing trees, but monkeys are better at swinging from branch to branch.

# Families

We see many kinds of families. Some families are big. Other families are small.

Some families live together, but other families live apart. Some children live with their moms, while others live with their dads.

Families are alike in some ways. Families give us food to eat and give us clothes to wear. Our families also take care of us when we are sick. We get love from our families, too.

# Plants
## and the Seasons
by Margaret McNamara

## Table of Contents

| | |
|---|---|
| **Words to Think About** | 110 |
| **Introduction** | 111 |
| **Chapter 1** Plants in Fall | 112 |
| **Chapter 2** Plants in Winter | 113 |
| **Chapter 3** Plants in Spring | 114 |
| **Chapter 4** Plants in Summer | 115 |
| **Conclusion** | 116 |
| **Glossary** | 117 |

© Benchmark Education Company, LLC

# Words to Think About

**bud**

This bud will become a flower.

**dormant**

Some plants become dormant, or don't grow, in winter.

**grow**

This flower needs water to grow, or get bigger.

**plants**

Plants grow in many places.

**seasons**

Fall, winter, spring, and summer are the four seasons.

**temperature**

The temperature is cold when it snows.

# Introduction

Earth has four **seasons**, or times of the year. The seasons are fall, winter, spring, and summer.

Some **plants** change in each season when the **temperature** changes. Plants also change because the amount of sunlight changes.

fall

winter

summer

spring

Chapter 1

# Plants in Fall

Plants change during fall because they have less sunlight. Some leaves change color in fall.

Plants need sunlight to make their own food and to **grow**. Farmers grow crops, or plants people use for food. Some crops are harvested, or picked, in fall. Other crops die in fall.

**Plant Fact**

Most pine trees stay green all year.

▲ The leaves on some trees change color.

corn

apples

pumpkins

▲ Corn crops die in fall. Farmers harvest apples and pumpkins in fall.

© Benchmark Education Company, LLC

Chapter 2

# Plants in Winter

During winter, plants get the least amount of sunlight. The temperatures are coldest.

Sometimes the ground is frozen and the roots of plants cannot get water. Many plants become **dormant** in winter. While a plant is dormant, it does not grow.

▲ The trees in this orchard are dormant.

sunflower

berries

▲ Some plants will grow again in spring. Some plants continue to grow in winter.

© Benchmark Education Company, LLC

113

Chapter 3

# Plants in Spring

Spring is warmer than winter. The warmer temperatures help plants grow. The ground can thaw, or become softer, and plants can get water again.

This season is when many plants grow **buds**. Some buds become leaves, but other buds become flowers.

**LOOK AT TEXT STRUCTURE**

**Compare and Contrast**

Some words can help you understand how things are alike and different. Find the word "than." This word is a clue that the author is comparing spring and winter. The word "but" is also a clue that the author is comparing. What is the author comparing?

▲ These apple trees have flowers in spring.

flower buds

leaf buds

flower buds

▲ Flowers and leaves begin as buds.

© Benchmark Education Company, LLC

Chapter 4

# Plants in Summer

Temperatures are warmest in summer and plants can get the most sunlight. The sunlight helps plants grow and bloom.

Some plants grow more leaves and flowers in summer. Farmers harvest some crops, such as corn.

**Did You Know?**
Some plants have fruit in summer.

corn

sunflowers

campanula

▲ Many plants have flowers in summer.

# Conclusion

Plants change in each season. Changes in temperature and the amount of sunlight affect plants.

fall
- harvest some crops
- some leaves change

winter
- some dormant plants

spring
- some buds

summer
- harvest some crops
- more leaves
- more flowers

# Glossary

**buds** new parts of plants

**dormant** not growing

**grow** to get larger

**plants** living things that make their own food and stay

**seasons** groups of months with the same weather

**temperature** how hot or cold something is

# Treasure Island?

An island is land with water all the way around it. Ships go by the island.

Sometimes things fall off the ships. The things float to the island. People find the things on the beach!

One island in the North Sea is Terschelling (ter-SKEL-ing). People may soon call it Treasure Island, though. Strange things are always floating to this island!

One time, people found sweaters on the beach. Another time, they found many pairs of tennis shoes. Another time they found children's toys. One November, a ship was in a storm. Tons of bananas fell off the ship and washed onto the beach.

People talked about the bananas. "They might be a little salty!" some people said.

"We could send them to a zoo!" said one man on the beach.

# Unit 9

## Table of Contents

A Summer Day . . . . . . . . . . . 120

Run, Fox, Run! . . . . . . . . . . 121

Kids Can Have Jobs . . . . . . . . . . 122

What Are Some Rules at School? . . . 123

Little Chick . . . . . . . . . . . . . 132

© Benchmark Education Company, LLC

# A Summer Day

It was a hot day, so Max got a bowl of ice cream. He sat outside to eat it.

Max's friend Lucy came by with her new puppy. Max put down his bowl so he could play with Lucy's puppy.

Max forgot all about his ice cream because he was busy playing with the puppy.

Max looked down. Oh no! The hot sun caused his ice cream to melt.

# Run, Fox, Run!

One crisp, clear morning three friends went hunting. Amy, Tom, and Tim had a box because they were planning to catch a fox. Quietly the friends waited and waited.

Then Amy called out, "Hey, we caught a fox!"

"He jumped right into the box!" said Tom.

"But look," Tim said. "The fox is crying."

"I think he wants to run," Amy said. "So we should let him go."

# Kids Can Have Jobs

Did you know kids can have jobs? Some kids deliver newspapers so people get the news.

Kids can feed their pets to help care for them.

Kids can shovel snow. When you move the snow off the sidewalk, then people won't slip and fall.

There are many jobs kids can do!

# What Are Some Rules at School?

by Margaret McNamara

## Table of Contents

| | |
|---|---|
| Words to Think About | 124 |
| Introduction | 125 |
| **Chapter 1** Rules Help You Learn | 126 |
| **Chapter 2** Rules Keep You Safe | 127 |
| **Chapter 3** Rules Teach Respect | 128 |
| **Chapter 4** Rules Help You Take Care of Your School | 129 |
| Conclusion | 130 |
| Glossary | 131 |

© Benchmark Education Company, LLC

# Words to Think About

**citizens**

These students are good citizens.

**community**

People work and play together in our school community.

**respect**

We show respect for others by reading quietly.

**rules**

This poster shows us the rules, or things we need to do.

**safe**

Walking, instead of running, keeps us safe.

**school**

School is a place to learn.

# Introduction

All good **citizens**, or members of a **community**, follow **rules**. Rules tell people what they should and shouldn't do.

Your **school** is a community. Your school has rules. In this book, you'll learn about rules at school.

▲ People need to follow rules in school.

## Chapter 1

# Rules Help You Learn

Students learn best when they get to school on time and pay attention. They also need to do their homework.

Teachers make rules so you will do these things. They want you to do your best in school.

**Rules at Your School**

What rules help you learn?

▲ This student follows a rule about doing homework.

Chapter 2

# Rules Keep You Safe

If you run down the halls, then you can fall or bump into others. If you do a science experiment without wearing safety equipment, you can get hurt.

Schools make rules so that you don't get hurt. The rules tell you how to be **safe**.

**Rules at Your School**

What rules keep you safe?

▲ Goggles keep your eyes safe during an experiment.

**Chapter 3**

# Rules Teach Respect

Good citizens treat others with **respect**. If you tease other students, then you are not showing respect. You show respect when you wait your turn to speak.

Schools want you to be a good citizen. They make rules to teach you respect.

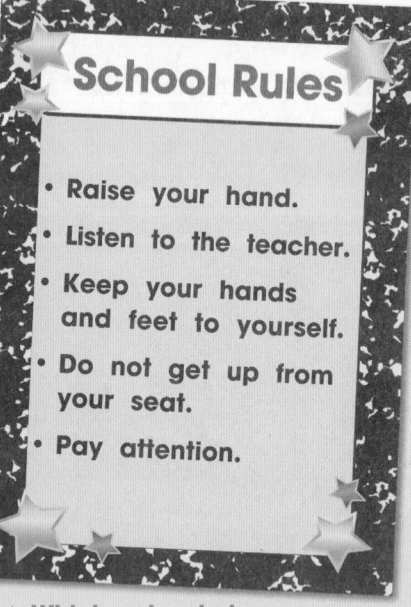

### School Rules

- Raise your hand.
- Listen to the teacher.
- Keep your hands and feet to yourself.
- Do not get up from your seat.
- Pay attention.

▲ Which rules help students show respect?

**LOOK AT TEXT STRUCTURE**

**Cause and Effect**

The word "if" shows a cause. The cause is teasing other students. The word "then" shows the effect.

© Benchmark Education Company, LLC

## Chapter 4

# Rules Help You Take Care of Your School

Many people work, learn, and play at your school. Everyone needs to take care of the school, too.

Some rules tell you how to keep the school clean. Some rules tell you how you can make the school better.

**Rules at Your School**

What rules help you take care of your school?

## Conclusion

Your school is a community. When you follow rules at school, you are a good citizen.

Rules at school help you learn, stay safe, and respect others. Rules help you take care of the school, too.

**Why Do We Follow Rules at School?**

# Glossary

**citizens** the people who are part of a community

**community** a place where people work and play together

**respect** care and concern for others

**rules** guides for what must happen

**safe** not getting hurt

**school** a place that people go to learn

# Little Chick

Hen got up and counted her chicks. "Little Chick is gone!" she said. "Oh no, oh no!"

Hen ran to the barn. "Horse! Horse! Have you seen Little Chick?" she asked.

"No," said Horse. "Go ask Rabbit if he has seen her."

Hen ran to the field. "Rabbit! Rabbit! Have you seen Little Chick?"

"No," said Rabbit. "Has Frog seen her? Go ask him."

Hen ran to the pond. "Frog! Frog! Have you seen Little Chick?"

"Yes," said Frog. "She went to the pigpen with Little Pig."

Hen ran to the pigpen. Little Chick was playing with Little Pig. "Little Chick!" cried Hen.

Little Chick looked up. "Oh, were you looking for me?" she asked.

# Unit 10

## Table of Contents

Ann's Party . . . . . . . . . . . . . . . 134

Ocean Animals . . . . . . . . . . . . . 135

Who Lives in a Forest? . . . . . . . . 136

Plants in Their Habitats . . . . . . . . 137

One Misty, Moisty Morning . . . . . . 146

# Ann's Party

"Can we have a party?" asked Ann.

"Yes!" said Mom. "Who will come?"

"A lion will come," said Ann.

"A lion?" asked Mom.

"A princess will come," said Ann.

"A princess?" asked Mom.

"A pirate, a cowboy, and a penguin will come, too!" said Ann.

"What kind of a party is it?" asked Mom.

# Ocean Animals

Some animals live deep in the ocean. Tube worms live so deep there is no light.

Other animals live near the top of the ocean. Dolphins are close to the top. Sometimes they jump out!

Still other ocean animals live on the sand. Crabs live in shells near the ocean's edge.

# Who Lives in a Forest?

A forest is a home for many plants. Trees live in a forest. Flowers and grasses live in a forest, too.

Many animals live in a forest. Birds live in a forest. Porcupines and bears also live in a forest.

Have you seen insects in a forest? Ants crawl along the trees and on the forest floor.

# Plants
## in Their Habitats

by Debra Castor

## Table of Contents

| | |
|---|---|
| **Words to Think About** | 138 |
| **Introduction** | 139 |
| **Chapter 1** Surviving Near a Pond | 140 |
| **Chapter 2** Surviving in a Tropical Rain Forest | 141 |
| **Chapter 3** Surviving in a Desert | 142 |
| **Chapter 4** Surviving in the Arctic | 143 |
| **Conclusion** | 144 |
| **Glossary** | 145 |

# Words to Think About

**dry**

The soil on the left is dry. The soil on the right is moist.

**habitats**

Plants live in many habitats.

**plants**

Earth has many types of plants.

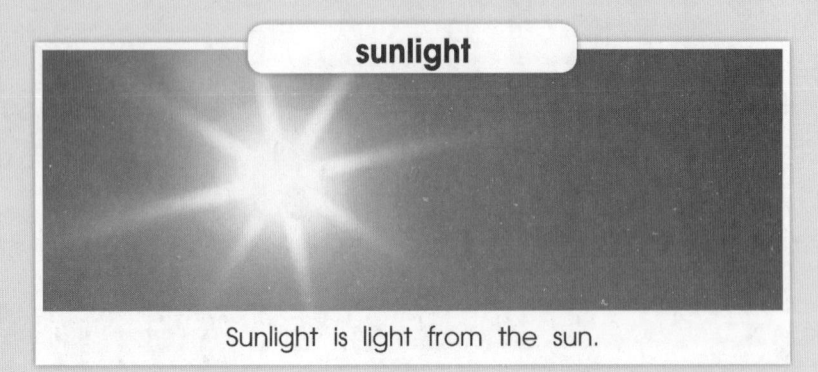

**sunlight**

Sunlight is light from the sun.

**survive**

Plants survive, or stay alive, in many habitats.

**water**

Plants need water to survive.

# Introduction

**Plants** live in many different **habitats**. Plants need **water**, air, light, and a place to grow.

Many plants have adapted, or changed, to **survive** in their habitats. This book shows some ways plants have adapted.

▲ Plants live where they can get the right amounts of water, air, light, and space.

**Chapter 1**

# Surviving Near a Pond

Plants that grow in and near ponds must be able to get the water, sunlight, and oxygen they need to survive. Cattails have parts that grow above and below the water.

The underwater roots absorb water, nutrients, and oxygen. The tall, sturdy leaves above the water absorb sunlight and oxygen.

tall, strong leaves

water lilies

lotus

water platters

▲ Cattails survive near this pond.

▲ These big water platters can get a lot of sunlight.

Chapter 2

# Surviving in a Tropical Rain Forest

A tropical rain forest is a very warm and wet habitat with many plants. The canopy layer of the rain forest blocks most **sunlight** from getting to the forest floor.

Vines have special roots that help them climb trees to get more sunlight.

vines

epiphyte

banana tree

bromeliad

▲ These vines have adapted to get the sunlight they need to survive.

▲ A bromeliad catches water to help the plant survive.

© Benchmark Education Company, LLC

141

**Chapter 3**

# Surviving in a Desert

A desert is a very **dry** habitat. Some plants, like cactuses, survive with very little water.

Cactuses have thick stems that hold water. The thick stems help cactuses survive in the dry desert.

thick stems

poppies

barrel cactuses

beavertail cactuses

**LOOK AT TEXT STRUCTURE**

**Description**

Find the word "dry." The author uses this word to describe the desert. What other words does the author use to describe things?

▶ Water is inside the thick stems of these saguaro cactuses.

▲ These plants survive with very little water.

142

© Benchmark Education Company, LLC

# Chapter 4

## Surviving in the Arctic

The Arctic is a very cold and windy habitat. How do plants survive in this habitat?

Bearberry plants grow close to the ground and have thick, tough leaves. These leaves protect the plant from cold temperatures and strong winds.

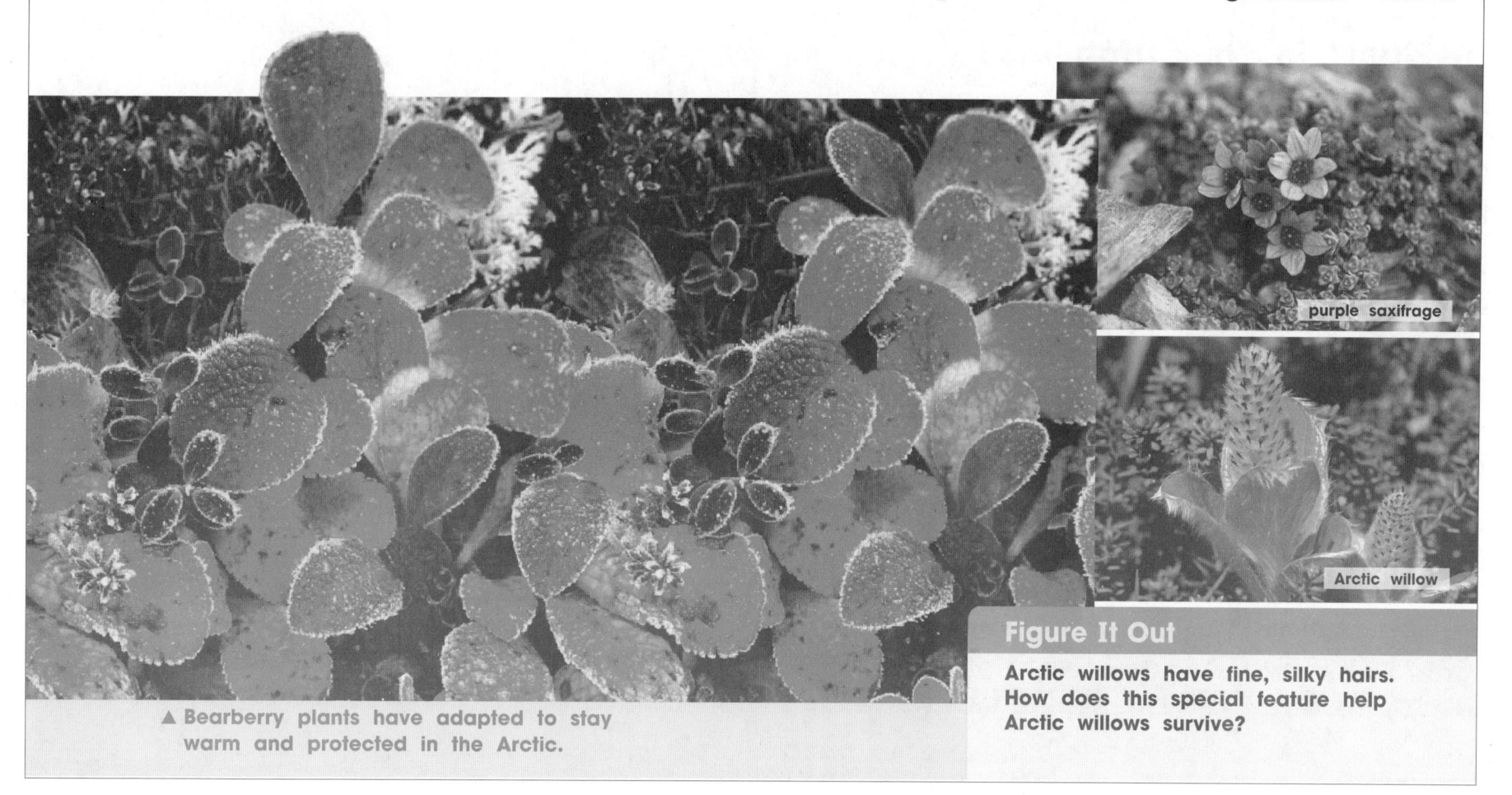

▲ Bearberry plants have adapted to stay warm and protected in the Arctic.

purple saxifrage

Arctic willow

### Figure It Out

Arctic willows have fine, silky hairs. How does this special feature help Arctic willows survive?

© Benchmark Education Company, LLC

# Conclusion

Plants live in many different habitats. All plants need the same things to survive in their habitats.

Plants have adapted to stay alive in their habitats.

## Plants in Their Habitats

**pond**

**cattails**
- parts that grow above and below the water

**tropical rain forest**

**vines**
- special roots

**desert**

**cactuses**
- thick stems

**the Arctic**

**bearberry plants**
- thick, tough leaves

# Glossary

**dry** very little water

**habitats** places where plants and animals live

**plants** living things that make their own food and stay in one place as they grow

**sunlight** light from the sun

**survive** to stay alive

**water** a liquid that plants need to live

# One Misty, Moisty Morning

One misty, moisty morning,

when cloudy was the weather,

I chanced to meet an old man,

clothed all in leather.

He began to compliment

and I began to grin.

How do you do? And how do you do?

And how do you do again?